treasure

Fifty conversations with God

By Lisa Bruton

WestBow Press books may be ordered through booksellers or by contacting:

WestBow Press
A Division of Thomas Nelson & Zondervan
1663 Liberty Drive
Bloomington, IN 47403
www.westbowpress.com
844-714-3454

Cover and interior art by Elisa Faith
Edited by Rebecca Gollan

ISBN: 979-8-3850-2341-7 (sc)
ISBN: 979-8-3850-2342-4 (hc)

Library of Congress Control Number: 2024907676

Print information available on the last page.

WestBow Press rev. date: 07/03/2024

WESTBOW
P R E S S®
A DIVISION OF THOMAS NELSON
& ZONDERVAN

"You welcome me as an honoured guest and fill my cup to the brim."

psalms 23:5

Hi Beautiful,

In your hands rests a book that will become your treasure. This book has been created to record life-changing conversations between you and God. Conversations that connect and entwine your heart to His. It will be a treasure of love letters, encouragement, revelations, fresh ideas, and blueprints from heaven.

It delights God to chat and spend time with you. God will speak and reveal wonders you did not know. There will be confirmations and affirmations. He will surprise you with answers to questions you have stopped asking. You will know beyond a shadow of a doubt just how abundantly loved you are.

Within this book there is a tapestry of questions woven together to offer a launching place into conversations with God. Some of the questions will evoke wonder and delight in Him. Other questions will require courage to go deep. Some questions will invite you to look at things that may have been buried for some time. Some questions will be a whole lot of fun.

This book of treasure has been intentionally designed with two pages per question. The first page is to record God's answers the first time you ask Him each question. The second page is to record the second time you ask Him the question. The book has been purposely created this way so that once you and God have completed the 50 heavenly conversations together you can go back and begin the questions again. You may want to begin the questions a second time straight away or you may be prompted to engage with the questions again in another season. This is your book and your precious conversations with God. Trust when He prompts you to begin the questions a second time.

As you ask these questions the second time you will see how God has led you forward. Some answers the second time may be similar but deeper, others will show you just how far you've journeyed with Him. It is a place to celebrate the break-throughs that have taken place, and a reminder of the treasure you hold and the treasure you are to Him.

This book isn't intended to produce any pressure to perform, strive or stress over whether or not God will speak. He will. He promises that He will respond. Jeremiah 33:3 says, "Call to me and I will answer you and tell you great and unsearchable things you do not know" (NIV). As you ask God a question, know He will answer you. You may find He gives you an impression. He may place a word or phrase strongly on your heart. He may use your imagination and show you a picture. He may speak to you through a thought you have. You may recall a scripture or a song that repeats over and over in your mind. God is so creative and knows just how you are wired. Trust what rises. Trust the simplicity and ease as He answers in a way that is so personal and unique to you.

As you ask the questions, write down the first thing that you hear, sense, and perceive. The Holy Spirit will partner with you as you write, and you will find at times there will be such a flow that reveals more than you could have imagined. Try to put your logical and practical mind aside as you record the answers. It's best not to censor or shake off what you hear because it doesn't make sense in the moment. God is fun and sometimes His answers may surprise you, but they are always perfect. I encourage you to simply begin to write what you hear and sense and allow the Holy Spirit to flow through your pen.

There is no correct way to enjoy this book. It is designed for you to go at your own pace. You can spend one day on a question, complete a few questions in a day, or enjoy sitting with one question over an entire week. You can skip a question (or questions) and come back when you are ready. This is your treasure trove with God. Now is a time to get to know God's heart for you. It's a time of healing, a time of wonder, a time of laughter, a time of feeling so deeply and completely loved. It is a time of delighting in God and Him in you. There is no striving, no pressure to perform and no stress to get it right. It is going to be fun. It will delight your heart.

The time spent with this book will help you realise just how fiercely loved you are and how incredibly valuable you are to the Father. So relax, find a space that you feel safe and comfortable in, and begin your treasured conversations with God.

Love Lisa xx

To support your treasured journey of conversations with God, a simple and beautiful audio has been created for each question. If you want to listen to the audio version of the questions, scan the code below and select the question you are wanting to ask.

Know God delights in you, and your heart is safe with Him. He is going to meet you in extraordinary ways. Have fun!

1. Father, how do You like spending time with me?

_____

_____

_____

_____

_____

_____

_____

_____

_____

_____

_____

_____

_____

_____

_____

_____

Treasure

2. Father, what miracles have You done in my life recently that I haven't noticed or realised?

_____

_____

_____

_____

_____

_____

_____

_____

_____

_____

_____

_____

_____

_____

_____

_____

_____

Treasure

5

3. Father, what lie am I believing about myself? What is the truth?

_____

_____

_____

_____

_____

_____

_____

_____

_____

_____

_____

_____

_____

_____

_____

Treasure

4.   Father, what promises have I forgotten about or let go of? What promises are You inviting me to pick up again in this season?

_____

_____

_____

_____

_____

_____

_____

_____

_____

_____

_____

_____

_____

_____

_____

_____

_____

5. God, what lie am I believing about You? What is the truth?

_____

_____

_____

_____

_____

_____

_____

_____

_____

_____

_____

_____

_____

_____

_____

_____

_____

_____

6. God, today can You display or show Your love for me?

Keep your eyes and ears open and aware. He is going to display the splendour of His love for you!

Psalm 119:124: Let me feel your tender love, for I am yours. (TPT)

_____

_____

_____

_____

_____

_____

_____

_____

_____

_____

_____

_____

_____

_____

_____

_____

Treasure

7. God, in what areas of my life do I worry about what others think of me? What do You say about these areas of my life?

_____

_____

_____

_____

_____

_____

_____

_____

_____

_____

_____

_____

_____

_____

_____

_____

_____

_____

Treasure

8.   Father, what promises have You fulfilled that I haven't realised or stopped to acknowledge?

Psalm 119:140: All your promises glow with fire … (TPT)

_____
_____
_____
_____
_____
_____
_____
_____
_____
_____
_____
_____
_____
_____
_____
_____
_____
_____
_____

Treasure

9.   God, what areas of my life do I have a limited expectation on how You will move, heal, show up or impact? What are You saying about this area in my life?

Matthew 9:29b: ... "You will have what your faith expects!" (TPT)

_____

_____

_____

_____

_____

_____

_____

_____

_____

_____

_____

_____

_____

_____

_____

_____

_____

_____

10. Father, is there someone I need to forgive? I hand them to You, God, and forgive them for … (be specific and can be more than one thing) and I pray a blessing over them. God, what do You give me in exchange?

_____

_____

_____

_____

_____

_____

_____

_____

_____

_____

_____

_____

_____

_____

_____

_____

Treasure

"You have captured our attention and the eyes of all who look to You.

You give what they hunger for at just the right time." Psalms 145:15

11. Father, what have I done recently that has made You really proud?

_____

_____

_____

_____

_____

_____

_____

_____

_____

_____

_____

_____

_____

_____

_____

_____

Treasure

12. God, what scripture are You drawing my attention to? What is it about this scripture I am to focus and dwell on today?

_____

_____

_____

_____

_____

_____

_____

_____

_____

_____

_____

_____

_____

_____

_____

_____

_____

_____

_____

Treasure

13. God, is there something in my life that I am trying to do in my own strength? Why am I trying to do these things in my own strength? I surrender these things to You Lord. What does it look and feel like when I am doing these things from a place of rest in You?

_____

_____

_____

_____

_____

_____

_____

_____

_____

_____

_____

_____

_____

_____

_____

_____

_____

14. Father, who do You want me to encourage today? How do You want me to encourage them?

_____

_____

_____

_____

_____

_____

_____

_____

_____

_____

_____

_____

_____

_____

_____

_____

Treasure

15. God, what promise or promises are You wanting me to embrace and believe for in this season?

Psalm 119:122: Let me hear your promises of blessing over my life ... (TPT)

_____

_____

_____

_____

_____

_____

_____

_____

_____

_____

_____

_____

_____

_____

_____

_____

_____

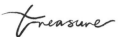

16. God, is there something in my life that feels dry or weighty? What do You say about those dry and weighty things?

_____

_____

_____

_____

_____

_____

_____

_____

_____

_____

_____

_____

_____

_____

_____

_____

_____

Treasure

17. Father, is there something specific You are inviting me to pray for today?

_____

_____

_____

_____

_____

_____

_____

_____

_____

_____

_____

_____

_____

_____

_____

_____

_____

Treasure

18. God, what have I done recently that gave You a good laugh?

_____

_____

_____

_____

_____

_____

_____

_____

_____

_____

_____

_____

_____

_____

_____

_____

_____

Treasure

19. God, how many people am I allowing to speak into my life right now? Is there anyone who is not meant to be speaking into my life in this season? God, have I positioned You to be the most influential voice in my life?

_____

_____

_____

_____

_____

_____

_____

_____

_____

_____

_____

_____

_____

_____

_____

_____

20. What song are You singing over me today, Lord?

God is speaking to you through a song today. Pay attention to songs, a chorus, a phrase of a song that you keep repeating. What is God speaking to you through songs?

"Come to me. I will refresh your life, for I am your oasis."

Matthew 11:28-30

21. Father, who are the two or three friends who are safe to have close that I can share my heart with?

_____

_____

_____

_____

_____

_____

_____

_____

_____

_____

_____

_____

_____

_____

_____

_____

Treasure

22. God, what intimidates me? Why does it intimidate me? What do You say about this, God?

_____

_____

_____

_____

_____

_____

_____

_____

_____

_____

_____

_____

_____

_____

_____

_____

_____

_____

23. God, are there areas in my life that I am "toning down" or downplaying? Why am I doing that? God, are You inviting me to shine brightly in these areas?

Treasure

24. Father, what is it about me that brings You delight?

_____

_____

_____

_____

_____

_____

_____

_____

_____

_____

_____

_____

_____

_____

_____

25. God, what are Your top three priorities for my life right now?

_____

_____

_____

_____

_____

_____

_____

_____

_____

_____

_____

_____

_____

_____

_____

_____

Treasure

26. God, what burden am I carrying that belongs to You? I place this burden back in Your hands God and trust You with the outcome. What do You give me in exchange?

_____

_____

_____

_____

_____

_____

_____

_____

_____

_____

_____

_____

_____

_____

_____

_____

_____

_____

Treasure

27. God, what part of Your nature is in me? What characteristics of Yours have You designed me with? How do I reflect You to the world?

Genesis 1:27: So God created mankind in his own image, in the image of God he created them... (NIV)

_____

_____

_____

_____

_____

_____

_____

_____

_____

_____

_____

_____

_____

_____

_____

_____

_____

Treasure

28. Father, what is something that You are inviting me to pause to acknowledge and celebrate today? How shall I celebrate it with You?

_____

_____

_____

_____

_____

_____

_____

_____

_____

_____

_____

_____

_____

_____

_____

_____

_____

_____

_____

Treasure

29. God, what lie am I believing about my future? What is the truth?

_____

_____

_____

_____

_____

_____

_____

_____

_____

_____

_____

_____

_____

_____

_____

_____

Treasure

30. God, what is Your definition of success for my life? What does Your success look like? I exchange my ideas of success for Your true definition of success.

_____

_____

_____

_____

_____

_____

_____

_____

_____

_____

_____

_____

_____

_____

_____

_____

_____

_____

Treasure

Treasure

31. Father, what do You love watching me do? Why?

_____

_____

_____

_____

_____

_____

_____

_____

_____

_____

_____

_____

_____

_____

_____

_____

_____

_____

Treasure

32. God, are there any gifts on my life that I am not aware of or have forgotten about?

_____

_____

_____

_____

_____

_____

_____

_____

_____

_____

_____

_____

_____

_____

_____

_____

Treasure

33. God, in what areas of my life do I hold myself against an unrealistic measuring stick? Show me any areas of my life where I feel like I don't measure up, that I am not enough or believe that I am too much. I give that measuring stick to You in exchange for Your grace. Father, what do You say about me?

34. God, what prophetic word do You want me to use as a weapon today?

1 Timothy 1:19: … use your prophesies as weapons as you wage spiritual warfare by faith and with a clean conscience (TPT).

_____

_____

_____

_____

_____

_____

_____

_____

_____

_____

_____

_____

_____

_____

_____

_____

_____

35. God, are there distractions in my life that are preventing me from focusing on the right things? What are the main things You want me to focus on right now?

_____

_____

_____

_____

_____

_____

_____

_____

_____

_____

_____

_____

_____

_____

_____

_____

_____

36. Father, is there something that I have been beating myself up about? Is there something I need to give myself grace for or forgive myself for?

_____

_____

_____

_____

_____

_____

_____

_____

_____

_____

_____

_____

_____

_____

_____

_____

37. Father, what passions have You placed within me? What brings delight and joy to my heart? Are these passions, delight and joy a part of my life at the moment?

_____

_____

_____

_____

_____

_____

_____

_____

_____

_____

_____

_____

_____

_____

_____

_____

_____

_____

38. God, can You show me a picture of me in the future?

Allow God to use your imagination to provide an image of you in the future. Write or draw the first image that comes to mind. Trust it is from Him. How does it make you feel? Does it make you uncomfortable? Excited? Delight? Challenged? Write that down too.

_____

_____

_____

_____

_____

_____

_____

_____

_____

_____

_____

_____

_____

_____

_____

_____

_____

39. God, is there something that is affecting my peace or a niggle that something isn't right? What do You want to show me about this? Help me to discern what is impacting my peace.

_____
_____
_____
_____
_____
_____
_____
_____
_____
_____
_____
_____
_____
_____
_____
_____
_____
_____

40. Father, how do I sense Your presence? What is the unique way You reveal Your presence to me?

If you haven't felt His presence before, ask Him to reveal His presence to you right now.

_____

_____

_____

_____

_____

_____

_____

_____

_____

_____

_____

_____

_____

_____

41. Father, show me any places in my heart that have become hard. What do You want to do in these areas of my heart?

_____

_____

_____

_____

_____

_____

_____

_____

_____

_____

_____

_____

_____

_____

_____

_____

_____

_____

42. What blessings and favour have You recently poured on my life, God?

_____

_____

_____

_____

_____

_____

_____

_____

_____

_____

_____

_____

_____

_____

_____

_____

_____

_____

Treasure

43. Am I discouraged about something God? What do You say about this discouragement? Can You encourage me today?

_____

_____

_____

_____

_____

_____

_____

_____

_____

_____

_____

_____

_____

_____

_____

_____

_____

_____

Treasure

44. God, what is it about me that makes You smile?

_____

_____

_____

_____

_____

_____

_____

_____

_____

_____

_____

_____

_____

_____

_____

_____

_____

_____

45. God, what false responsibility am I carrying for others? What do You say about this false responsibility, God? I hand that responsibility back to You. Lord, can You show me what is my responsibility towards this person?

46. What new thing are You drawing my attention to, God?

_____

_____

_____

_____

_____

_____

_____

_____

_____

_____

_____

_____

_____

_____

_____

_____

_____

_____

Treasure

47. What do You say about me today God?

_____

_____

_____

_____

_____

_____

_____

_____

_____

_____

_____

_____

_____

_____

_____

_____

_____

48. God, what is something fun we can do together? When shall we go have that fun, God?

_____

_____

_____

_____

_____

_____

_____

_____

_____

_____

_____

_____

_____

_____

_____

_____

Treasure

49. God, are there doors of opportunity and connections You are opening? Is there anything I need to do to walk through these open doors?

_____

_____

_____

_____

_____

_____

_____

_____

_____

_____

_____

_____

_____

_____

_____

_____

_____

50. Father, is there a frustration I have in regard to Your timing? Is there something I believe should have taken place already? What do You say about Your timing?

_____

_____

_____

_____

_____

_____

_____

_____

_____

_____

_____

_____

_____

_____

_____

_____

In your hands rests a book that will become your treasure. Inside are fifty questions that offer a launching place into conversations with God. Some questions will evoke wonder, others will require courage — but all are crafted to help you deepen your relationship with God and go further on your journey with Him.

The book is designed for you to go at your own pace. You can spend one day on a question, complete a few questions in a day, or enjoy sitting with one question over an entire week. You can skip a question (or questions) and come back when you are ready. The time spent with this book will help you realise just how fiercely loved you are and how incredibly valuable you are to the Father.

Lisa Bruton is a speaker, podcaster, and founder and director of Arise Sanctuary, an organisation that offers luxury boutique retreats for women in locations around the world. She is passionate about creating spaces for others to slow down, connect to God and hear His voice. Lisa has spoken at conferences and churches throughout Australia and overseas, where she openly shares her heart, funny mishaps, lessons and revelations. Lisa is a wife to Matty and mum to two young girls, Aria and Coco. In her spare time, she loves to surf and travel with her family.